INDEPENDENCE

Photographs by DAN WHITE

Text by BRENT SCHONDELMEYER

B.J.P., Inc./Independence, Missouri
1985

INDEPENDENCE

was photographed by Dan White,
written by Brent Schondelmeyer,
designed by David E. Spaw, Spaw & Associates, Inc.,
photocomposed in Palatino
and printed on 80-pound Lustro Offset Enamel—
a neutral pH paper with an expected 300-year library
storage life as determined by the
Council of Library Resources of the
American Library Association—
by The Lowell Press,
115 East 31st Street, P. O. Box 1877,
Kansas City, Missouri 64141.

These photographs of Independence, Missouri, were taken during a six-month period in 1985. All photographs by Dan White except the Vaile Mansion, page 14, Donald A. Potts.

Most photographs were taken with Canon F-1s using lenses from 20-mm to 500-mm and Kodachrome 64 film. The other photographs were taken with either a Hasselblad or a Linhof view camera. The Linhof was used for the portraits on pages 4, 12, 20, 28, 37 and the Truman Home interiors.

Special thanks to Nick Vedros and Associates for their technical assistance.

The cover photograph, also found on page 19, contains items generously provided by the Jackson County Historical Society from their Archives and Research Library and the 1859 Marshal's House and Jail Museum, both located on the Independence Square.

FIRST EDITION

Text Copyright © 1985 by B.J.P., Inc.

Photographs Copyright © 1985 by Dan White

Library of Congress Catalog Card Number 85-72740

ISBN 0-932845-00-2 (hard cover)   0-932845-09-6 (soft cover)

All rights reserved. No part of this book may be reproduced, stored in a retrieval system, or transmitted in any form or by any means, electronic, mechanical, photocopying, recording or otherwise, without the prior written permission of the publisher and the photographer.

Published by B.J.P., Inc./Independence, Missouri

Opposite page: The Truman statue on the Independence Square.

"Boy, it was wild the day after that [1948 presidential] election. It really was. Nothing was done, nothing. We had a parade. I couldn't believe it. Well, I believed that the results would be that way, but the rest of the people couldn't believe it. But then they were enthused because Mr. Truman was from Independence. . . . I had $30 at 15-1 with one of the [pharmacists]. That was $450. The next day . . . he brought the money in, in cash, and I bought a phonograph-radio combination cabinet in mahogany."

PETEY CHILDERS

INDEPENDENCE

Its very name reflected important ideas of the new nation—freedom of thought, freedom of religion, a chance to make a future on the frontier.

In 1827, the town founders cleared a tract of Missouri woodlands near an Indian path and several clearwater springs for a new county seat and named the place Independence. The town to the north already had been named Liberty.

For more than 150 years, Independence, Missouri, has been making history. Few towns in the United States of comparable size can claim a history as rich and varied as Independence's.

From its town square, thousands of pioneers headed West. A charismatic religious leader designated the city as a spiritual center for Mormonism. During the Civil War, brother fought brother on the city streets. And during World War II, a plain-speaking, hometown boy, Harry Truman, made the peace.

A town, though, is something more than its past. Today the future of the town can be seen in its people, in the farm fields, on the factory lines, in the church pews, at school, at play and in the homes of its residents. Twice the city has been selected an All-America City by the National Municipal League.

But within that rich history, it was Truman who made the town an indelible part of the nation's conscience. The pundits helped. They made the president's hometown a part of his name—Harry Truman, "The Man from Independence."

Longtime residents, when prompted, can spin endless stories about life in "old Independence"—a small town with electric streetcars, Easter parades, Saturday nights when the farmers came to town for haircuts and nickel movie theaters. Most have a story or two about Harry and Bess Truman, who

Petey Childers and his wife, Drusilla, have been lifetime Independence residents and spent almost 50 years living on Main Street.

grew up and attended school in Independence and shared more than 50 years of married life in a house at 219 North Delaware Street.

Only after his death in December 1972 did the community honor Truman with a statue. Truman insisted on "no monuments to the living." The statue—a 9-foot bronze by sculptor Gilbert Franklin—depicts the 5'9" Truman striking out on a brisk walk. (The statue, located on the east side of the Jackson County Courthouse, was dedicated on Truman's May 8 birthday anniversary in 1976 with President Gerald Ford present.)

Each May the city awards an outstanding American the Harry S. Truman Public Service Award during ceremonies at the Truman Library. The recipients include Jimmy Carter, Hubert Humphrey, Henry Kissinger, Averell Harriman, Coretta Scott King and

The Truman portrait, a favorite of Bess Truman, hangs in the Trumans' living room. It was painted in 1945 by Missouri-born artist Jay Wesley Jacobs. The kitchen is in the original circa 1850 portion of the house, which was home to four generations of Bess Wallace Truman's family. She willed the presidential home to the United States. It was on the porch that the Trumans indulged in favorite pastimes: Harry Truman would pore over several newspapers and Bess would have friends over and play bridge.

Margaret Truman Daniel, the Trumans' daughter who grew up in the Delaware Street house.

That home reflects the Trumans' taste and their living habits. There is the back porch, the brightly-colored kitchen, the family piano and the informal study where Harry read history and biographies, while Bess, sitting alongside, was engrossed in a good mystery. Extensive research has established that the earliest portions of the home were built probably between 1848 and 1850. A major remodeling was completed in 1885.

It became the Trumans' private home and remained so until Bess died in 1982 at age 97, having lived longer than any other First Lady. Occasionally, the Trumans would entertain friends or host politicians. Each person to become United States president since Truman has visited Independence.

Truman's daily routine included a walk. He would head out the side door, grab his cane and walk

Even after he had died, Harry Truman's hat and umbrella continued to hang by the side door—the exit he normally used to walk from his house to the Truman Library located a mile to the north on U.S. 24 Highway. The library entrance is dominated by a well-known mural, "Independence and the Opening of the West," painted by Thomas Hart Benton.

the short mile to the Truman Library, which was dedicated in 1957. The Trumans are buried in the library courtyard.

The presidential library is primarily about Truman, his policies and interpretative exhibits about the presidency.

Truman's remarkable 30-year career in public service began in 1922 at the Jackson County Courthouse. There Truman picked up from a fellow county politician the phrase: "If you can't stand the heat, get out of the kitchen." In 1933, Truman had the courthouse remodeled in a style reminiscent of Independence Hall in Philadelphia. The present courthouse incorporates portions of an 1828 foundation—the first permanent courthouse.

The courthouse, though it receives little official use, contains Truman's restored county office. The strong association between Independence and the former president has been a magnet pull on the mind of America, drawing to the city thousands of visitors as well as the powerful, anxious to stand in Truman's shadow.

Court no longer is held on the second floor of the Jackson County Courthouse, but each Friday courtships culminate in quiet informal wedding ceremonies. The courthouse is the scene for a leisurely lunch or a frequent setting for politics and presidents.

11

*"We have childhood memories about going to grandma's, going to aunts and uncles and their old big houses. We **live** in the old house. Those fond memories that you have of the family picnics and the reunions—we don't have to go anywhere. We can have the old house and create those memories."*

ELLEN MORRIS

Independence once literally was on the western frontier. Today it is part of Middle America by location and also community values.

There is a resurgence of "old" city reflected in growing community interest in preserving and restoring older buildings. Harry Truman helped.

In November 1971, a year before his death, the ailing president gave the United States Department of the Interior his approval to designate a 12-block area around his Delaware Street home as a National Historic Landmark District. It is one of approximately 1,600 historically or culturally important areas nationwide so honored.

The heightened interest in the Truman neighborhood spurred other restoration efforts elsewhere in the city.

Opposite page: Ellen Morris, who along with her husband, Terry, moved from Texas to Independence. They bought and restored a century-old home on Delaware Street where they live with their daughters Meg and Molly.

Both the Vaile Mansion and the Bingham-Waggoner Estate—listed on the National Register of Historic Places—are being restored to some of their previous grandeur through the work of master craftsmen. The restoration work is guided by extensive historical research into original room colors, materials and building methods employed during earlier building and remodelings. Plans for the Vaile Mansion are to make it a museum facility concerned with Victorian culture. Its century-old ceiling painting, being restored, was originally done by European-born artisans brought by Harvey Vaile to work on his home. The Second Empire style with its mansard roof makes the Vaile Mansion the more interesting of the two structures architecturally. The style of the Bingham-Waggoner is Italianate Renaissance Revival.

The Bingham-Waggoner home is a footnote in American art history. The building was the home (1864-1870) of painter George Caleb Bingham, whose keen interest in Missouri life and politics resulted in several well-known paintings. It was at his Independence home that Bingham, though sympathetic to the Union cause, painted his famous scene, commonly known as "Order No. 11." That order, given by a Union general in 1863, resulted in martial law and the forcible removal of many western Missouri residents from their land—a scene that Bingham depicted. Of the infamous order that enraged his artistic furor, Bingham later said: "The effect of it was not only the depopulation, but the desolation of one of the fairest and most highly cultivated districts in our state. The people, indiscriminately, were compelled to abandon their homes—men, women, and children. Their dwellings were plundered and then burned to the ground." The artist's actual studio on the estate was demolished. The music room would have been part of the house during Bingham's time, though may have been used as a dining room or a second parlor. Major additions were made to the home in 1899. The building, which is open for tours, also is used extensively for wedding receptions, parties and other social functions.

Frontier Independence was caught up in the major historical developments and events of the nineteenth century.

The city entertained explorers and mountain men; steamboats and wagon trains; gold miners and homesteaders; a civil war and religious strife.

The land on which Independence was founded became part of the United States through the 1803 Louisiana Purchase from France. For $15 million, the United States acquired, sight unseen, more than 800,000 square miles.

The extensive journals of Meriwether Lewis and William Clark included some of the first detailed descriptions of land that now is part of Independence—the Little Blue River valley. The explorers stopped there in 1804 to pick plums, raspberries and wild apples. They also spotted bears and several deer.

It would be another two decades before permanent settlers established Jackson County and in turn made Independence its county seat.

The new town was well situated to take advantage of the growing trade with Santa Fe, then a part of Mexico. The first Santa Fe trading trips originated in Franklin, Missouri, in 1821; but the skill of steamboat pilots moved the trailhead farther west and upstream.

In 1832, a Missouri River steamboat landing was established near Independence. The city was located near the bend in the river where the muddy 2,700-mile tributary turned northward.

Starting out from Independence cut the time and the distance it took to reach Santa Fe. The steamboat ride from St. Louis cost about $6 and took nearly a week. Another two months were needed to cover the 800-mile overland trip to Santa Fe.

Independence boomed. It was the Queen City of the nation's new western empire. One county census counted more blacksmiths than teachers, tailors, tanners, telegraphers and tobacconists combined.

By 1842, attention turned to Oregon. The homesteaders followed the Santa Fe Trail to Gardner, Kansas. There the Oregon-bound wagons went northwest to the Platte River, westward through Nebraska, over the Rocky Mountains at the 29-mile wide South Pass in Wyoming and on to Oregon.

Fortune seekers during the 1849 California Gold Rush followed the Oregon Trail into Idaho where the California Trail turned southwest.

There were two basic ways at that time to reach the West. One was the expensive, long, hazardous ocean journey. Overland was the other route.

There were only 2,000 miles of railroad in the entire United States in 1838 with no tracks crossing the Great Plains. Wagon trains were replaced by steam engines with the completion of a transcontinental railroad in 1869.

The westward expansion funneled the nation's new pioneers through a few Missouri River towns. Many of the 290,000 persons who made the overland journey between 1840 and 1860 bought their goods, filled their water barrels, hitched their teams and set out from Independence on the three-month overland journey to California or Oregon.

Opposite page: They are items of a pioneer past: a wagon jack, a wagon wheel, sturdy boots, utilitarian burlap and a couple who were among the earliest settlers in the area.

Independence recalls its role in the westward expansion with a Labor Day weekend celebration on the Independence Square called Santa-Cali-Gon Days after the Santa Fe, California and Oregon trails.

But the community and state sought a more permanent expression of the community's Three Trails heritage by creating a first-class museum dealing with the westward expansion.

The site for the trails center is a two-story brick warehouse that was part of the Waggoner-Gates Milling Co. Wagon trains used to cross the land on their way out of town. At a later date, George Porterfield Gates became a partner in the milling business and built a fine home at 219 North Delaware Street. His granddaughter Bess and her husband Harry Truman would eventually live there.

Not all was peace and prosperity in the frontier town. The issue of slavery divided Independence as it did the nation.

Independence's first settlers came mostly from Kentucky, Tennessee, Virginia and the Carolinas. Many brought with them slaves who worked as tradesmen, domestics or field hands, who farmed hemp, corn, oats and tobacco. Of Independence's 3,100 permanent residents in 1860, nearly one-fourth were black.

Southern sympathies in the town were strong, though sentiments were opposed to secession from the Union.

There was a brief battle around the Independence Square in August 1862 that resulted in more than 75 soldiers being killed or wounded. The courthouse was used as a hospital.

Then on October 21, 1864, Confederate troops commanded by Gen. Sterling Price battled a Union force that had taken up ground on the western bank of the Little Blue River. Eventually, the Union troops retreated to Independence where a house-to-house battle ensued.

The Union forces withdrew from Independence that night to join the troops who were dug in along the Big Blue River farther west. The Confederate troop advance was halted that week in the Battle of Westport—an engagement that involved more than 29,000 soldiers.

Union and Confederate soldiers who died in Independence are buried in separate sections of Woodlawn Cemetery where their graves are marked with flags every Memorial Day.

The Civil War was not the first time the town had been up in arms. Thirty years earlier, the community drove hundreds of "Mormons" out of town.

At the time, a dynamic new religion was developing in the United States under the leadership of Joseph Smith. In 1830, Smith sent leaders to frontier Independence to conduct missionary work with nearby Indians.

In just two years about 1,200 church members had moved to Independence. One factor behind the mass migration was Smith's prophecy that Independence someday would be the site of the Second Coming.

Opposite page: The memory of the Civil War lingers. Local residents reenact the period with historically authentic uniforms, equipment and mock battles.

The "Mormon" influx into Independence rankled established settlers, who feared a shift in political power, the loss of business to church members and were bothered by the abolitionist tendencies of the church members. Persecution of the Mormons resulted in violence on both sides.

By July 1833, town leaders formally asked the Mormons to leave Independence. That winter the Mormons, en masse, crossed the Missouri River to settle in Liberty. Many of their Independence homes were burned to the ground.

The grassy triangular-shape of ground is known as the "Temple Lot" because it is the site that Mormon prophet Joseph Smith dedicated in August 1831 for construction of a temple—an event marked by a small monument. Adjacent to the Temple Lot is the domed world headquarters of the 225,000-member Reorganized Church of Jesus Christ of Latter Day Saints and the Mormon Visitors' Center operated by the Church of Jesus Christ of Latter-day Saints in Salt Lake City, Utah.

23

Organ lovers know the instrument simply as "The Auditorium Organ"—the name of the radio program that since 1960 has featured the Aeolian-Skinner organ in the conference chamber of the world headquarters of the Reorganized Church of Jesus Christ of Latter Day Saints. The weekly half-hour program, hosted by organist John Obetz, is available to all National Public Radio and fine arts stations throughout the United States. From a four-manual console, organists can change the timbre of the music by playing keys that electrically allow air through various combinations of the 6,000 handmade pipes that range in length from one-quarter inch to 32 feet. The dome is nearly 100 feet high. The diameter of the elliptical free-span dome is 214 feet at its widest point. There are several community musical groups and talented musicians such as the violinist who plays his handmade instrument.

25

The early pioneers brought their prayers and Bibles to the frontier. Not long after the town was settled, permanent churches were established by Protestants, Roman Catholics and the Latter Day Saints. Religion continues to be a major force in the community today. Two churches, both founded in the 1860s, are the focal point for the 800-member black community. Many are descendants of former Independence slaves. Three older churches are on the National Register of Historic Places. They are: the First Presbyterian Church where six-year-old Harry Truman first laid eyes on a year younger blue-eyed blonde named Bess Wallace during Sunday School; the Trinity Episcopal Church where the two were married in 1919 at the respective ages of 35 and 34; and the Church of Christ-Temple Lot, located on the lot that Mormon prophet Joseph Smith dedicated for a temple.

"The community accepted us pretty well. . . . It's just a place to live, but I think it's pretty nice."
VIA PEOLA

A city is its people: the young and the old; the homegrown kid and the transplant; the native-born and the foreigner; the professional and the blue-collar worker. It is also those people long since gone that bestowed on the community a sense of place and purpose drawn from the community's rich history. Independence is no longer on the frontier; in fact, it is part of a 1.5 million Kansas City metropolitan area. Independence, with a population of 110,000, is the fourth largest city in the state of Missouri and one of only about 175 communities nationwide that are larger than 100,000.

The city maintains strong sister city relationships with two communities— Higashimurayama, Japan and the African city of Blantyre, Malawi. Japanese gardeners from the sister city spent weeks planting a "Friendship Garden" at city hall.

Opposite page: Via, the teenage daughter of Ruth Peola, who moved her family to Independence from the South Pacific nation of Western Samoa.

29

The walls of the community center used to resound with the roar of electric turbines generating power for city residents since the 1930s. But during the late 1970s the former municipal power plant was adapted to a new use: a city-operated community center named after former mayor Roger T. Sermon. The sounds that fill the building now are those of dribbling basketballs, actors delivering lines during city theater productions, senior citizens exchanging words while dancing cheek-to-cheek at big band dance nights and the quietude of a checker player pondering his next move.

34

35

"My wife Dorothy and I discovered Independence in the autumn of 1955 and chose this community to make our home. We shared the thrill of creative efforts which have afforded fine friendships and abundant business opportunities."

LU VAUGHAN

Independence displays the diversity of the American economy as a whole. There are factories, yet family-owned farms; shopping centers, yet neighborhood stores; century-old buildings, yet modern architecture; crowded industrial areas, yet wide-open space suitable for development. Most residents work outside the city, though community plans anticipate developing the eastern portion of the city as a major industrial area.

Lu Vaughan, a successful businessman, who opened one of the first twin drive-in theaters in the country.

37

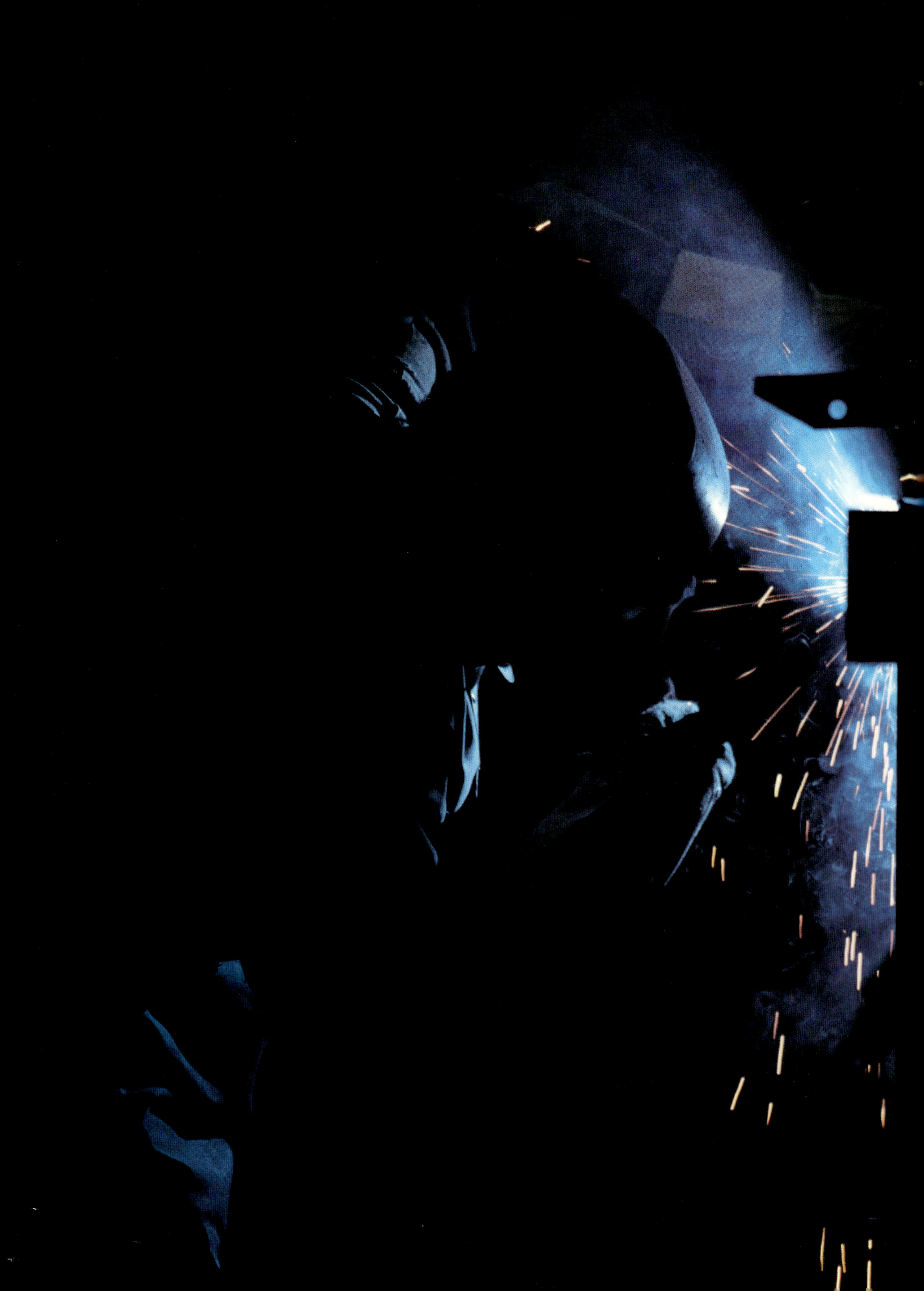

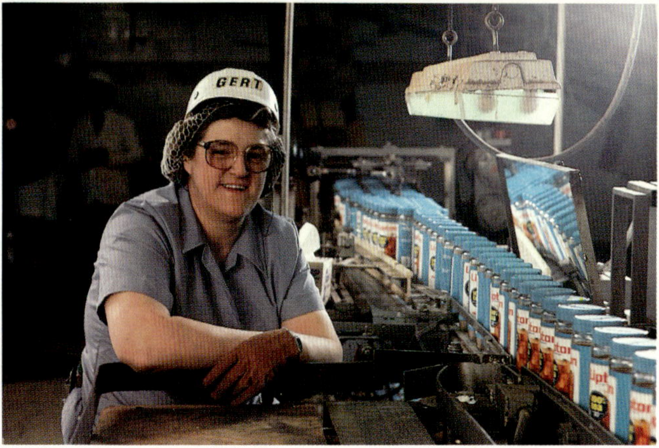
GERT

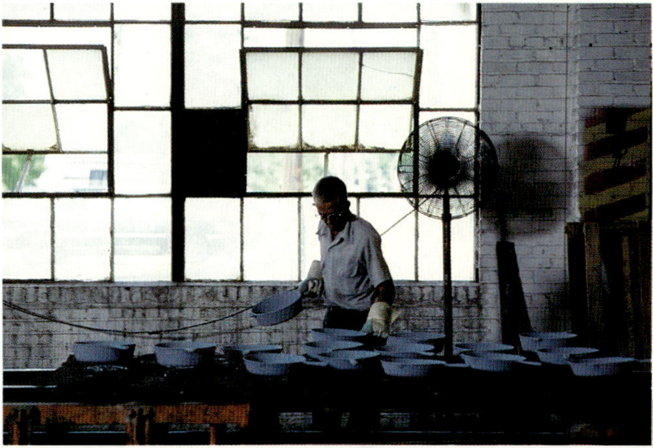

40

Previous pages: The city has a variety of manufacturing concerns. There are foundry operations, a munitions plant and manufacturers, such as Deutz-Allis where metal is stamp-pressed and welded into combines and Thomas J. Lipton, Inc., which makes salad dressing and tea for nationwide distribution.

Once a rural lane that divided the corn fields, Noland Road is a classic example of urban strip development. Consumers now daily harvest fast foods, cars, clothes, computers and other merchandise along a five-mile stretch. But not all is the hustle-bustle of the great neon-lit roadway. Brown bags and neighborhood bars are still part of the working life for blue-collar workers.

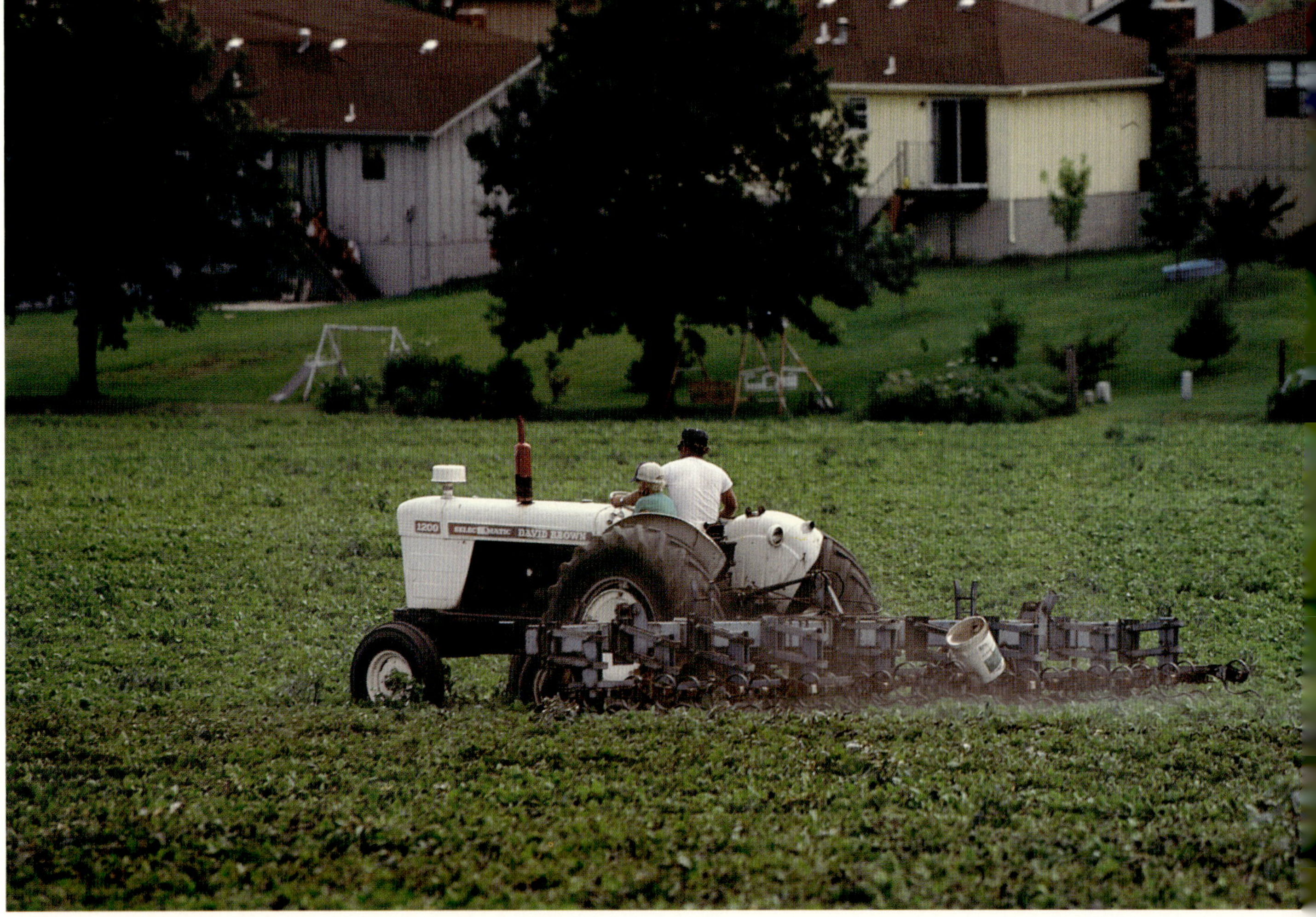
1200
DAVID BROWN

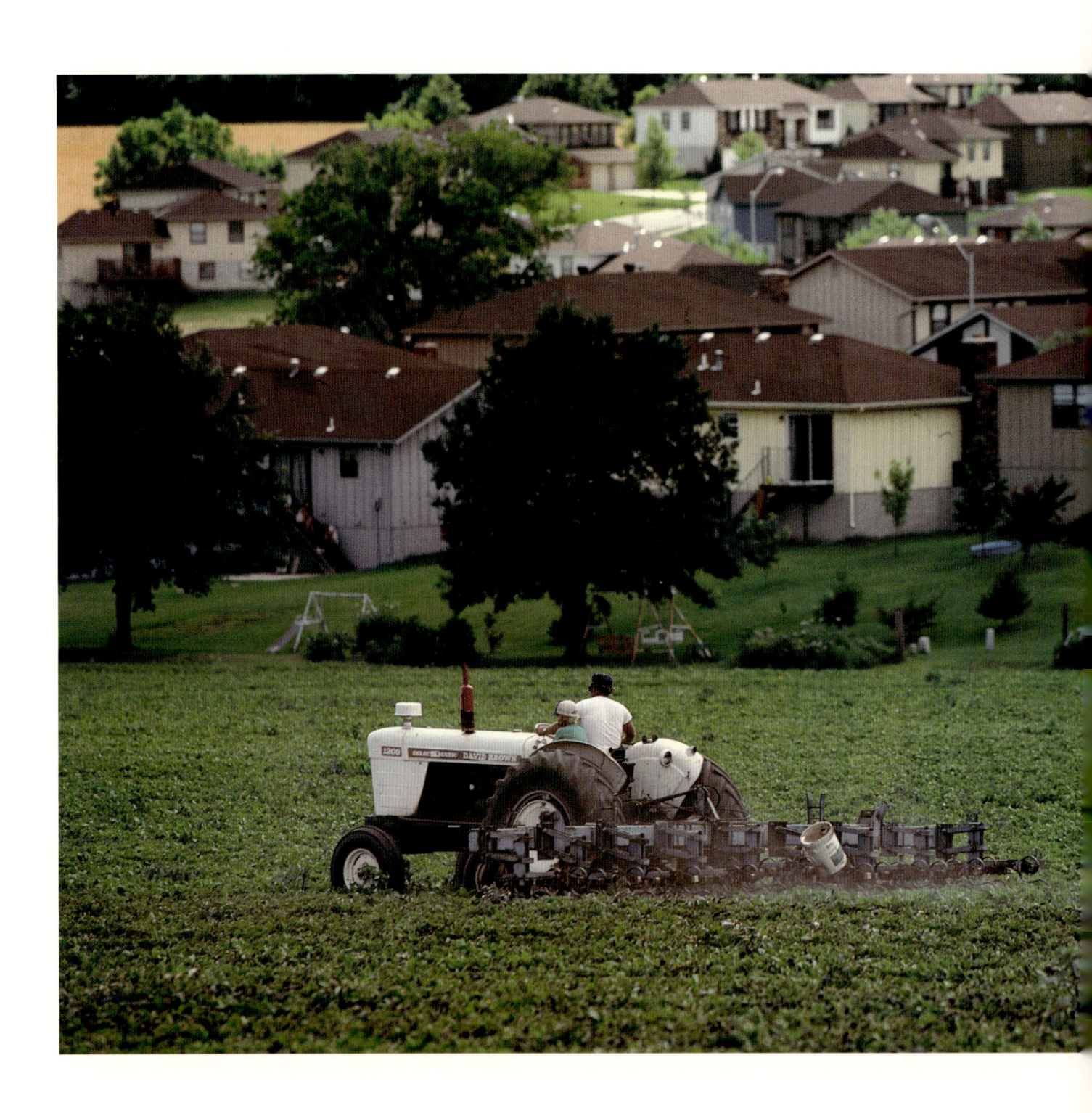

The community has strong ties to agriculture, though many farmland acres have become suburban housing developments. "City" farmers plant, plow and harvest soybeans, corn and winter wheat. There is a farmer's market on the Independence Square where fresh produce—apples, peaches, corn, cabbage, rhubarb and other fruits and vegetables—are sold out of the back of pickup trucks and station wagons by those who grew them.

Following pages: The city does not stop where the housing ends. More than one-third of the city's total area is in the Little Blue River valley which is largely agricultural, though some areas are considered prime sites for major industrial development.

43

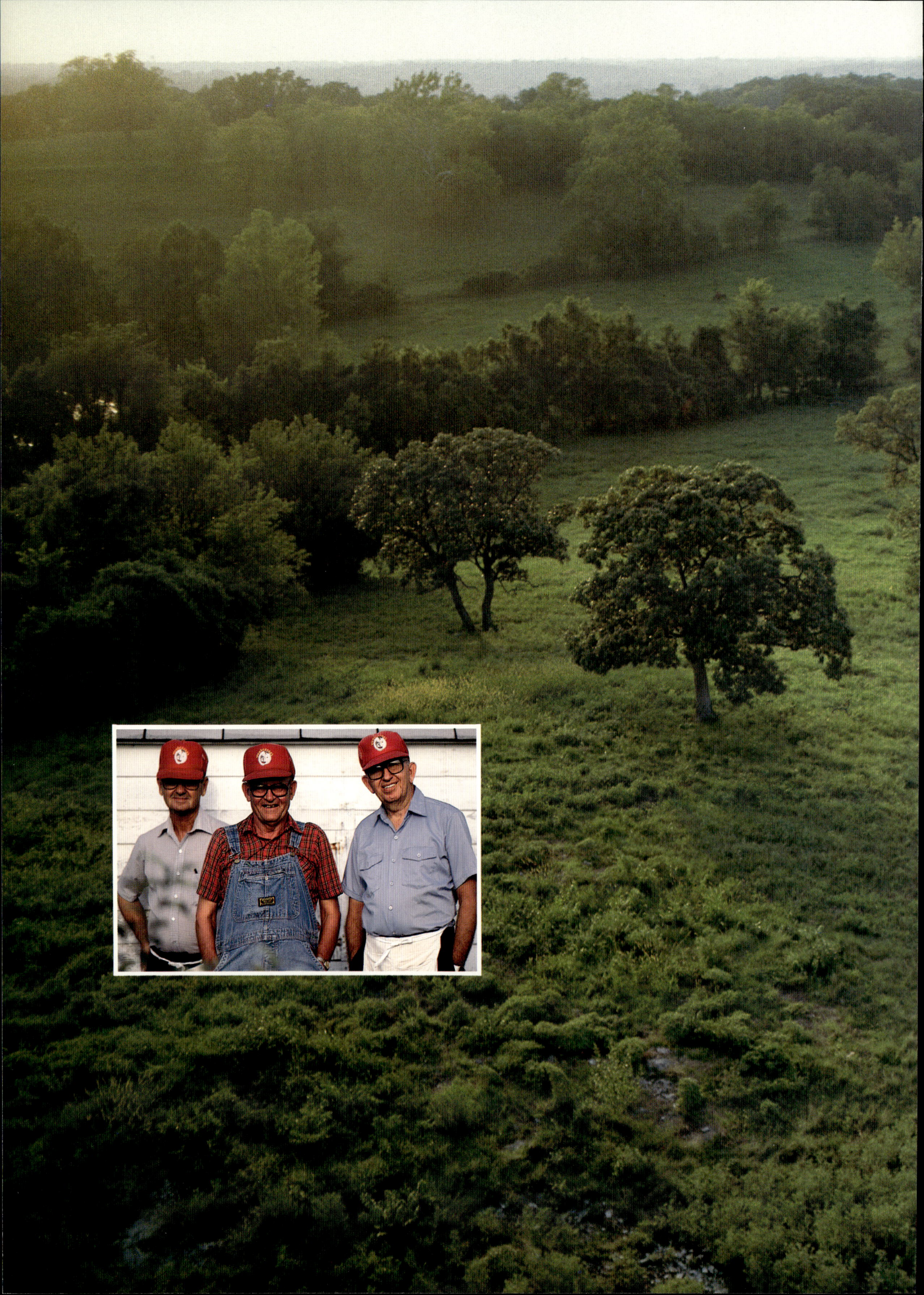

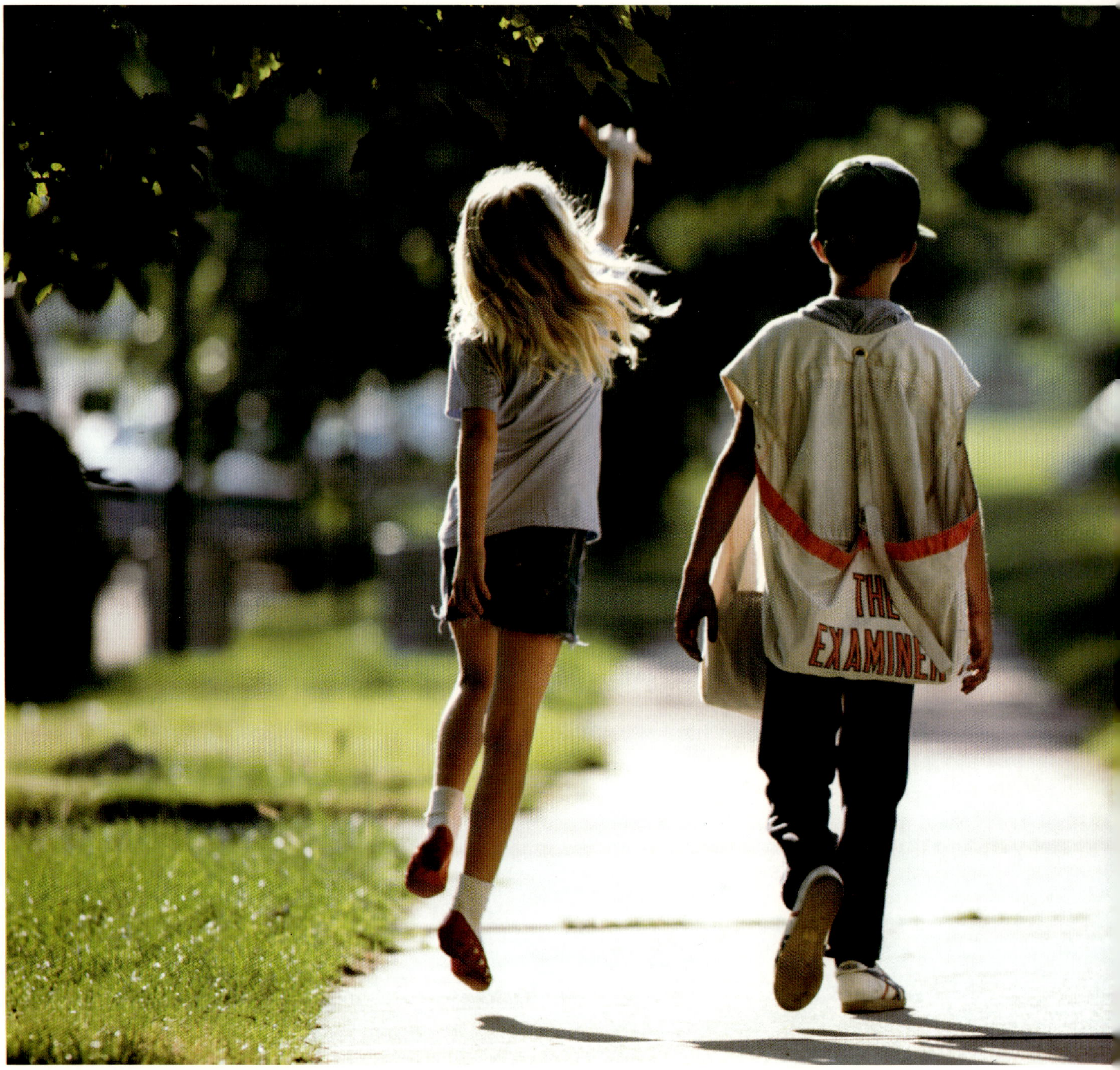
THE
EXAMINER

This book reflects my deep affection for the people of Independence:

The people of yesterday who laid the foundation of our rich heritage;

The people of today who are good neighbors and friends;

The people of tomorrow for whom planning and building continues. I hope this book touches you in some personal way, whether you have lived in Independence a lifetime or merely visited for a day. Many of these pictures could have been taken anywhere. But others are special and unique to our community.

Perhaps something in these pages makes you smile, see a familiar site in a new way, "remember when" or think briefly about what it means to be a community—regardless of where you call home.

To my hometown, thank you Independence for opening your homes, your churches, your schools, your businesses and your hearts to make this book possible.

BARBARA J. POTTS

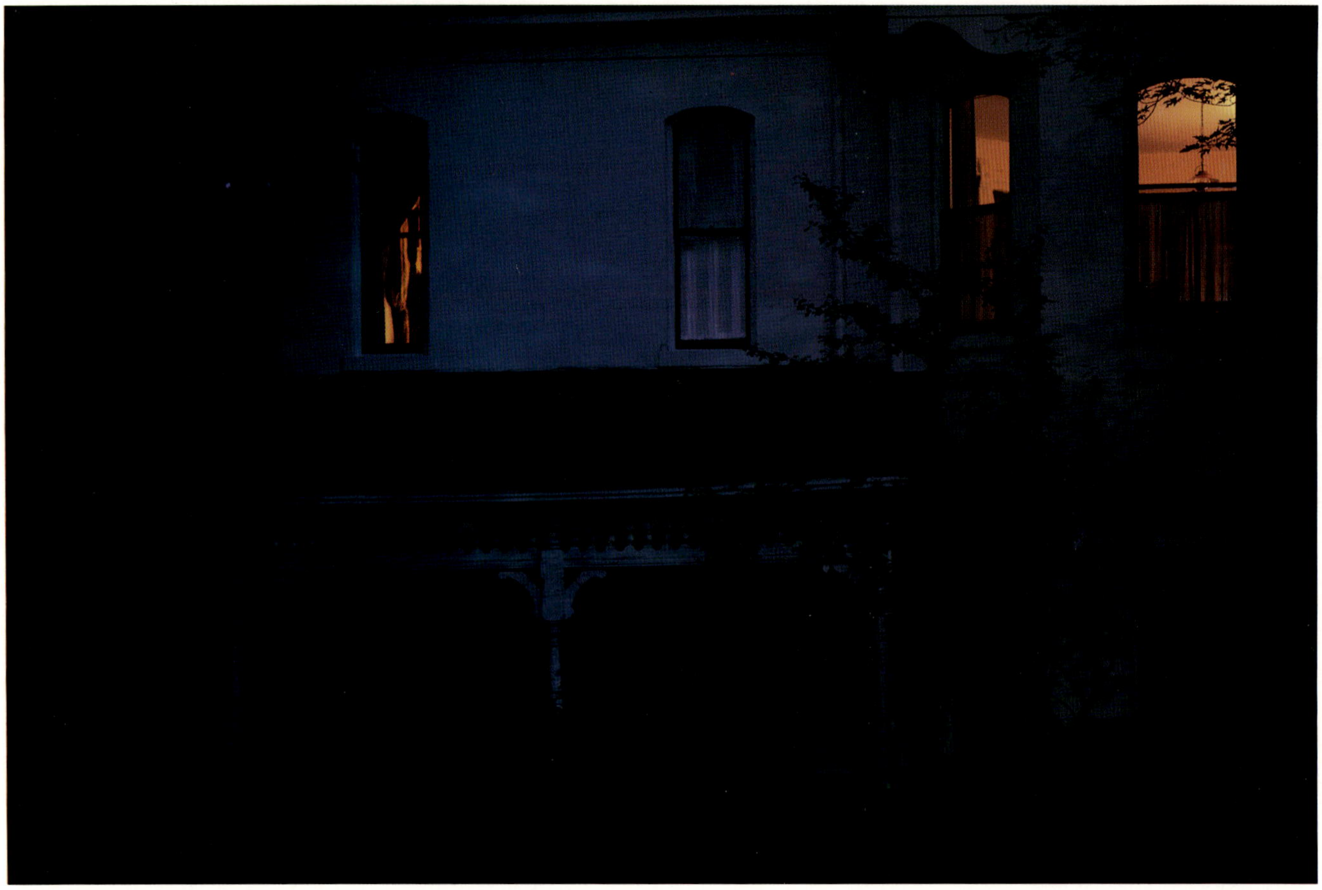